EASY CREPE COOKBOOK

50 DELICIOUS CREPE RECIPES

By
Chef Maggie Chow
Copyright © by Saxonberg Associates

Published by
BookSumo, a division of Saxonberg Associates
http://www.booksumo.com/

INTRODUCTION

Welcome to *The Effortless Chef Series*! Thank you for taking the time to download the *Easy Crepe Cookbook*. Come take a journey with me into the delights of easy cooking. The point of this cookbook and all my cookbooks is to exemplify the effortless nature of cooking simply.

In this book we focus on Crepes. You will find that even though the recipes are simple, the taste of the dishes is quite amazing.

So will you join me in an adventure of simple cooking? If the answer is yes (and I hope it is) please consult the table of contents to find the dishes you are most interested in. Once you are ready jump right in and start cooking.

— Chef Maggie Chow

TABLE OF CONTENTS

ANY ISSUES? CONTACT ME

If you find that something important to you is missing from this book please contact me at maggie@booksumo.com.

I will try my best to re-publish a revised copy taking your feedback into consideration and let you know when the book has been revised with you in mind.

:)

— Chef Maggie Chow

LEGAL NOTES

COMMON ABBREVIATIONS

cup(s)	C.
tablespoon	tbsp
teaspoon	tsp
ounce	oz.
pound	lb

*All units used are standard American measurements

CHAPTER 1: EASY CREPE RECIPES

SIMPLE CREPES

Ingredients

- 1 C. all-purpose flour
- 2 eggs
- 1/2 C. milk
- 1/2 C. water
- 1/4 tsp salt
- 2 tbsps butter, melted

Directions

- In a large bowl, add the eggs and flour and beat till well combined.
- Slowly, add the water and milk, beating continuously till well combined.
- Add the butter and salt and beat till smooth.
- Lightly, grease a frying pan and heat it on medium-high heat.
- Place about 1/4 C. of the mixture and tilt the pan to spread it evenly.
- Cook for about 2 minutes.
- Carefully, flip the crepe and cook till golden brown.
- Repeat with the remaining mixture.
- Serve hot.

Amount per serving (4 total)

Timing Information:

Preparation	10 m
Cooking	20 m
Total Time	30 m

Nutritional Information:

Calories	216 kcal
Fat	9.2 g
Carbohydrates	25.5g
Protein	7.4 g
Cholesterol	111 mg
Sodium	235 mg

* Percent Daily Values are based on a 2,000 calorie diet.

Sweet Crepes

Ingredients

- 4 eggs, lightly beaten
- 1 1/3 C. milk
- 2 tbsps butter, melted
- 1 C. all-purpose flour
- 2 tbsps white sugar
- 1/2 tsp salt

Directions

- In a large bowl, add all the ingredients and beat till well combined and smooth.
- Lightly, grease a crepe pan and heat on medium heat.
- Place about 3 tbsps of mixture and tilt the pan to spread it evenly.
- Cook for about 1-2 minutes per side.
- Repeat with the remaining mixture.
- Serve hot.

Amount per serving (8 total)

Timing Information:

Preparation	10 m
Cooking	10 m
Total Time	20 m

Nutritional Information:

Calories	164 kcal
Fat	7.7 g
Carbohydrates	17.2g
Protein	6.4 g
Cholesterol	111 mg
Sodium	235 mg

* Percent Daily Values are based on a 2,000 calorie diet.

BUTTERED VANILLA CREPES

Ingredients

- 1 1/2 C. milk
- 3 egg yolks
- 2 tbsps vanilla extract
- 1 1/2 C. all-purpose flour
- 2 tbsps sugar
- 1/2 tsp salt
- 5 tbsps melted butter

Directions

- In a large bowl, add the egg yolks, milk and vanilla and beat till well combined.
- Add the remaining ingredients and beat till smooth.
- Lightly, grease a crepe pan and heat on medium heat.
- Place about 1/4 C. of the mixture and tilt the pan to spread it evenly.
- Cook everything on both sides till golden brown.
- Repeat with the remaining mixture.
- Serve hot with a filling of your choice like ice cream, caramel, cheese, cream or fruit.

Amount per serving (12 total)

Timing Information:

Preparation	10 m
Cooking	20 m
Total Time	30 m

Nutritional Information:

Calories	142 kcal
Fat	6.7 g
Carbohydrates	15.9g
Protein	3.3 g
Cholesterol	66 mg
Sodium	146 mg

* Percent Daily Values are based on a 2,000 calorie diet.

Spiced Banana Filled Crepes

Ingredients

- 1 C. all-purpose flour
- 1/4 C. confectioners' sugar
- 2 eggs
- 1 C. milk
- 3 tbsps butter, melted
- 1 tsp vanilla extract
- 1/4 tsp salt
- 1/4 C. butter
- 1/4 C. packed brown sugar
- 1/4 tsp ground cinnamon
- 1/4 tsp ground nutmeg
- 1/4 C. half-and-half cream
- 6 bananas, halved lengthwise
- 1 1/2 C. whipped heavy cream
- 1 pinch ground cinnamon

Directions

- In a large bowl, sift together the powdered sugar, flour and salt.
- Add the milk, 3 tbsps of butter, eggs and vanilla and beat till smooth.
- Lightly, grease a skillet and heat on medium-high heat.
- Place about 3 tbsps of the mixture and tilt the pan to spread it evenly.
- Cook till golden brown and carefully, flip it.
- Cook till golden brown.
- In another large skillet, melt the remaining butter and stir in the brown sugar, nutmeg and 1/4 tsp of cinnamon.

- Repeat with the remaining mixture.
- Add the cream and cook, stirring continuously till the mixture becomes slightly thick.
- Add the banana slices, at one time and gently stir to coat with sauce.
- Cook for about 2-3 minutes and remove from heat.
- Place a banana slice in the middle of a crepe and roll it.
- Place the crepes onto serving plates and top with the cream from the pan.
- Serve immediately with a sprinkling of cinnamon.

Amount per serving (6 total)

Timing Information:

Preparation	5 m
Cooking	15 m
Total Time	20 m

Nutritional Information:

Calories	518 kcal
Fat	28.7 g
Carbohydrates	60.7g
Protein	8 g
Cholesterol	146 mg
Sodium	252 mg

* Percent Daily Values are based on a 2,000 calorie diet.

FRENCH STYLED CREPES

Ingredients

- 1 C. all-purpose flour
- 1 tsp white sugar
- 1/4 tsp salt
- 3 eggs
- 2 C. milk
- 2 tbsps butter, melted

Directions

- In a large bowl, sift together the white sugar, flour and salt.
- Add the milk and eggs and beat till smooth.
- Add the melted butter and stir to combine.
- Lightly, grease a skillet and heat on medium-high heat.
- Place about 2 tbsps of the mixture and tilt the pan to spread it evenly.
- Cook till golden brown and carefully, flip it.
- Cook till golden brown.
- Repeat with the remaining mixture.
- Serve hot.

Amount per serving (12 total)

Timing Information:

Preparation	5 m
Cooking	30 m
Total Time	35 m

Nutritional Information:

Calories	94 kcal
Fat	4.1 g
Carbohydrates	10.3g
Protein	4 g
Cholesterol	55 mg
Sodium	96 mg

* Percent Daily Values are based on a 2,000 calorie diet.

Vanilla Crepes

Ingredients

- 1 1/2 C. all-purpose flour
- 1 tbsp white sugar
- 1/2 tsp baking powder
- 1/2 tsp salt
- 2 C. milk
- 2 tbsps butter, melted
- 1/2 tsp vanilla extract
- 2 eggs

Directions

- In a large bowl, sift together the white sugar, flour, baking powder and salt.
- Add the remaining ingredients and beat till smooth.
- Place about 1/4 C. of the mixture and tilt the pan to spread it evenly.
- Cook for about 2 minutes and carefully, flip it.
- Cook till golden brown.
- Repeat with the remaining mixture.
- Serve hot.

Amount per serving (12 total)

Timing Information:

Preparation	15 m
Cooking	15 m
Total Time	30 m

Nutritional Information:

Calories	111 kcal
Fat	3.7 g
Carbohydrates	15g
Protein	4 g
Cholesterol	39 mg
Sodium	160 mg

* Percent Daily Values are based on a 2,000 calorie diet.

SOY MILK CREPES

Ingredients

- 1/2 C. soy milk
- 1/2 C. water
- 1/4 C. melted soy margarine
- 1 tbsp turbinado sugar
- 2 tbsps maple syrup
- 1 C. unbleached all-purpose flour
- 1/4 tsp salt

Directions

- In a large bowl, add all the ingredients and beat till smooth.
- Refrigerate, covered for at least 2 hours before serving.
- Lightly, grease a skillet and heat on medium-high heat.
- Place about 3 tbsps of the mixture and tilt the pan to spread it evenly.
- Cook everything on both sides till golden brown.
- Repeat with the remaining mixture.
- Serve hot.

Amount per serving (4 total)

Timing Information:

Preparation	5 m
Cooking	20 m
Total Time	2 h 25 m

Nutritional Information:

Calories	268 kcal
Fat	12.1 g
Carbohydrates	35.6g
Protein	4.3 g
Cholesterol	0 mg
Sodium	295 mg

* Percent Daily Values are based on a 2,000 calorie diet.

CREAMY CHOCOLATE CREPES

Ingredients

- 2 eggs
- 1/2 C. milk
- 1/2 C. water
- 3/4 C. all-purpose flour
- 6 tsps white sugar
- 1/3 tbsp butter
- 1 fluid ounce cognac
- 1 (3.9 ounce) package instant chocolate pudding mix
- 1 tsp instant coffee granules
- 3 C. heavy cream
- 4 (1 ounce) squares bittersweet chocolate
- 1/2 C. butter
- 1 1/4 C. nonfat evaporated milk
- 2 1/2 C. confectioners' sugar

Directions

- For the crepes,, in a large bowl, add the flour, white sugar, milk, eggs, water, cognac and 1/3 tbsps of butter and beat till smooth.
- For filling, in another bowl, add the instant coffee, heavy cream and pudding mix and beat till a thick and smooth mixture forms.
- Lightly, grease a skillet and heat on medium-high heat.
- Place the desired amount of mixture and tilt the pan to spread it evenly.
- Cook everything on both sides till golden brown.

- Repeat with the remaining mixture.
- Meanwhile For the sauce, in a small pan, add the evaporated milk, chocolate, confectioner's sugar and remaining butter and cook, stirring continuously till the mixture becomes slightly thick.
- Divide the filling into crepes and roll around the filling.
- Place the sauce over the crepes and serve.

Amount per serving (15 total)

Timing Information:

Preparation	1 m
Cooking	1 m
Total Time	2 m

Nutritional Information:

Calories	434 kcal
Fat	27.6 g
Carbohydrates	41.2g
Protein	5.1 g
Cholesterol	109 mg
Sodium	205 mg

* Percent Daily Values are based on a 2,000 calorie diet.

CRAB FILLED CREPES

Ingredients

Crepes:

- 2 C. flour
- 1 C. cold water
- 4 eggs
- 2 tbsps melted butter
- 1/2 tsp salt

Filling:

- 4 tbsps butter
- 1/2 C. chopped green onion
- 3/4 C. dry sherry
- 1/4 tsp salt
- 1/4 tsp ground black pepper
- 3 C. fresh crabmeat, cooked and diced

Sauce:

- 4 tbsps butter
- 6 tbsps all-purpose flour
- 2 C. hot milk
- 1/4 tsp salt
- 1/4 tsp ground black pepper
- 1/2 C. heavy cream
- 2 egg yolks
- 1 C. grated Swiss cheese

Directions

- For the crepes, in a large bowl, add all the ingredients and beat till smooth.
- Refrigerate, covered for at least 2 hours before serving.

- Lightly, grease a skillet and heat on medium-high heat.
- Place the desired amount of mixture and tilt the pan to spread it evenly.
- Cook everything on both sides till golden brown.
- Repeat with the remaining mixture.
- For the filling, in a skillet, melt 1/4 C. of butter on medium-high heat and sauté the green onions for about 3-5 minutes.
- Stir in the sherry and desired amount of salt and black pepper.
- Add the crab meat and stir to combine and remove from heat.
- Meanwhile for the sauce in a pan, melt the butter on medium-high heat.
- Slowly, add the flour, beating continuously till well combined.
- Add the milk, salt and black pepper and bring to a boil for about 1 minute.
- Meanwhile in a bowl, add the egg yolks and cream and beat till well combined.
- Remove the pan from heat and slowly, add the cream mixture, beating continuously till well combined.
- Fold in the Swiss cheese and reserve 1 C. of sauce in a bowl.
- Add the remaining sauce in the crab mixture and stir to combine.
- Divide the filling into crepes and roll around the filling.
- Place the sauce over the crepes and serve.

Amount per serving (8 total)

Timing Information:

Preparation	20 m
Cooking	30 m
Total Time	2 h 50 m

Nutritional Information:

Calories	542 kcal
Fat	33.4 g
Carbohydrates	37.7g
Protein	20.9 g
Cholesterol	234 mg
Sodium	699 mg

* Percent Daily Values are based on a 2,000 calorie diet.

QUINOA & HONEY CREPES

Ingredients

- 1 C. quinoa flour
- 1 C. almond milk
- 2 large eggs
- 1 tsp honey
- 1 pinch sea salt
- 2 tbsps melted butter

Directions

- For the crepes in a large bowl, add all the ingredients and beat till smooth.
- Lightly, grease a skillet and heat on medium-high heat.
- Place the desired amount of mixture and tilt the pan to spread it evenly.
- Cook everything on both sides till golden brown.
- Repeat with the remaining mixture.
- Serve hot.

Amount per serving (3 total)

Timing Information:

Preparation	15 m
Cooking	10 m
Total Time	25 m

Nutritional Information:

Calories	312 kcal
Fat	15.1 g
Carbohydrates	32.2g
Protein	11.2 g
Cholesterol	144 mg
Sodium	271 mg

* Percent Daily Values are based on a 2,000 calorie diet.

SEAFOOD FILLED CREPES

Ingredients

Cooking spray Crepes:

- 1 1/2 C. milk
- 3 eggs
- 1 1/4 C. all-purpose flour
- 1/4 tsp salt

Filling:

- 1 1/2 C. water
- 1/4 C. all-purpose flour
- 1/4 tsp salt
- 2 tbsps butter
- 4 cloves garlic, minced

- 2 pounds shrimp, peeled and deveined
- 8 ounces lobster meat
- 1 tbsp lemon juice
- 1 pinch cayenne pepper
- 1/4 C. grated Parmesan cheese

Sauce:

- 1 C. milk
- 2 tbsps mayonnaise
- 1 tbsp all-purpose flour

Directions

- Set your oven to 350 degrees F and grease a 12x9-inch baking dish.
- For the crepes in a large bowl, combine the eggs and milk and beat till frothy.
- Add the flour and salt and beat till smooth.

- Lightly, grease a griddle and heat on medium-high heat.
- Place about 1/4 C. of the mixture and tilt the pan to spread it evenly.
- Cook for about 4 minutes and carefully, flip it.
- Cook for about 2 minutes.
- Repeat with the remaining mixture.
- For the filling, in a bowl, add the flour and salt and beat till well combined and keep aside.
- In a nonstick skillet, add the butter and garlic on medium-low heat and cook, covered for about 7 minutes.
- Stir in the lobster and shrimp meat and cook, covered for about 5 minutes.
- Stir in the cayenne pepper and lemon juice and cook, covered for about 5 minutes more.
- Stir in the flour mixture and increase the heat to medium.
- Add the cheese and cook, stirring continuously for about 1 minute and remove from heat.
- Divide the filling into crepes and roll around the filling.
- Meanwhile for the sauce in a pan, add all the ingredients on medium heat and cook, stirring continuously for about 2-3 minutes.
- Place the crepe rolls into prepared baking dish in a single layer.
- Place the sauce over rolls evenly and cook in the oven for about 25-30 minutes.

Amount per serving (10 total)

Timing Information:

Preparation	30 m
Cooking	1 h
Total Time	1 h 30 m

Nutritional Information:

Calories	291 kcal
Fat	9.8 g
Carbohydrates	19.5g
Protein	29.5 g
Cholesterol	229 mg
Sodium	427 mg

* Percent Daily Values are based on a 2,000 calorie diet.

CARAWAY SEES CREPES

Ingredients

- 1 C. all-purpose flour
- 1 C. water
- 1 egg
- 2 tbsps butter, melted
- 1 pinch salt
- 1 tbsp caraway seeds

Directions

- In a large bowl, mix together the water and flour.
- Add the eggs and stir to combine.
- Add the butter, caraway seeds and salt and beat till smooth.
- Lightly, grease a griddle and heat on medium-high heat.
- Place about 1/4 C. of the mixture and tilt the pan to spread it evenly.
- Cook for about 2-4 minutes and carefully, flip it.
- Cook for about 30 seconds.
- Repeat with the remaining mixture.
- Serve hot.

Amount per serving (6 total)

Timing Information:

Preparation	10 m
Cooking	20 m
Total Time	30 m

Nutritional Information:

Calories	125 kcal
Fat	5 g
Carbohydrates	16.5g
Protein	3.5 g
Cholesterol	41 mg
Sodium	41 mg

* Percent Daily Values are based on a 2,000 calorie diet.

COFFEE SYRUP FOR THE CREPES,

Ingredients

- 2 tbsps brown sugar
- 1 1/2 tsps brewed coffee

Directions

- In a plate add the brown sugar and pour the coffee on top and stir to combine.
- Serve the crepes with coffee syrup.

Amount per serving (3 total)

Timing Information:

Preparation	5 m
Cooking	5 m
Total Time	10 m

Nutritional Information:

Calories	34 kcal
Fat	0 g
Carbohydrates	8.9g
Protein	0 g
Cholesterol	0 mg
Sodium	3 mg

* Percent Daily Values are based on a 2,000 calorie diet.

Yogurt & Jelly Filled Crepes

Ingredients

- 1 C. whole wheat flour
- 1 C. skim milk
- 4 egg whites
- 1 tbsp olive oil
- 1 tsp ground cinnamon

- olive oil cooking spray
- 1 C. plain fat-free Greek yogurt
- 1 tbsp jelly
- 1 pinch ground cinnamon

Directions

- In a large bowl, mix together the flour, 1 tsp of cinnamon, egg whites, milk and oil and beat till smooth.
- Lightly, grease a skillet and heat on medium-high heat.
- Place about 1/4 C. of the mixture and tilt the pan to spread it evenly.
- Cook for about 2 minutes and carefully, flip it.
- Cook for about 2 minutes.
- Repeat with the remaining mixture.
- In a bowl, mix together the jelly and yogurt.
- Spread a thin layer of the yogurt mixture over each crepe and roll it.
- Place the remaining yogurt mixture over the crepe rolls and serve.

Amount per serving (2 total)

Timing Information:

Preparation	10 m
Cooking	10 m
Total Time	20 m

Nutritional Information:

Calories	430 kcal
Fat	8.1 g
Carbohydrates	62.8g
Protein	29.6 g
Cholesterol	2 mg
Sodium	210 mg

* Percent Daily Values are based on a 2,000 calorie diet.

SPICED COCONUT CREPES

Ingredients

- 4 eggs, beaten
- 1/4 C. coconut flour
- 1/4 C. coconut milk
- 1 tbsp honey
- 1/4 tsp vanilla extract
- 1 pinch ground nutmeg
- 1 pinch ground cinnamon
- 1 tsp olive oil

Directions

- In a large bowl, add all the ingredients except oil and beat till smooth.
- Grease a crepe pan with olive oil and heat on low heat.
- Place about 1/4 C. of the mixture and tilt the pan to spread it evenly.
- Cook for about 30 seconds and carefully, flip it.
- Cook till golden brown.
- Repeat with the remaining mixture.
- Serve hot.

Amount per serving (6 total)

Timing Information:

Preparation	10 m
Cooking	10 m
Total Time	25 m

Nutritional Information:

Calories	126 kcal
Fat	7.2 g
Carbohydrates	10.4g
Protein	5.8 g
Cholesterol	124 mg
Sodium	48 mg

* Percent Daily Values are based on a 2,000 calorie diet.

Chocolaty Strawberry Filled Crepes

Ingredients

CREPES

- 1 egg, beaten
- 1/4 C. skim milk
- 1/3 C. water
- 1 tbsp vegetable oil
- 2/3 C. all-purpose flour
- 1/4 tsp white sugar
- 1 pinch salt

FILLING

- 1/2 C. semisweet chocolate chips
- 1 C. sliced fresh strawberries
- 3/4 C. frozen whipped topping, thawed

Directions

- For the crepes in a large bowl, add the milk, oil, egg and water and beat till well combined.
- Add the remaining ingredients and beat till smooth.
- Lightly, grease a griddle and heat on medium-high heat.
- Place about 1/4 C. of the mixture and tilt the pan to spread it evenly.
- Cook for about 2-5 minutes, flipping once.
- Repeat with the remaining mixture.

- For the filling, in a pan, add the chocolate chips on low heat and cook, stirring continuously till melted completely and remove from heat.
- Divide the melted chocolate in the center of the crepes, followed by strawberries and roll around the filling.
- Place the whipped topping over the crepes and serve.

Amount per serving (4 total)

Timing Information:

Preparation	5 m
Cooking	15 m
Total Time	10 m

Nutritional Information:

Calories	279 kcal
Fat	13.4 g
Carbohydrates	36.3g
Protein	5.4 g
Cholesterol	47 mg
Sodium	27 mg

* Percent Daily Values are based on a 2,000 calorie diet.

MILKY CREPES

Ingredients

- 2 C. milk
- 3/4 C. white sugar
- 2 C. all-purpose flour
- 2 eggs
- 1 tbsp baking powder
- 1 tsp vanilla extract
- 1 tsp vegetable oil

Directions

- In a blender, add all the ingredients except oil and beat till smooth.
- Lightly, grease a skillet and heat on medium heat.
- Place about 1/4 C. of the mixture and tilt the pan to spread it evenly.
- Cook everything on both sides till golden brown.
- Repeat with the remaining mixture.
- Serve hot.

Amount per serving (6 total)

Timing Information:

Preparation	10 m
Cooking	20 m
Total Time	30 m

Nutritional Information:

Calories	323 kcal
Fat	4.4 g
Carbohydrates	61.3g
Protein	9.1 g
Cholesterol	69 mg
Sodium	225 mg

* Percent Daily Values are based on a 2,000 calorie diet.

Egg-Free Crepes

Ingredients

- 1/2 C. skim milk
- 2/3 C. water
- 1/4 C. butter, melted
- 2 tbsps vanilla extract

- 1 C. all-purpose flour
- 1 tbsp white sugar
- 1/4 tsp salt
- 1 tbsp vegetable oil

Directions

- In a large bowl, add the butter, milk, water and vanilla and beat till well combined.
- In another bowl, mix together the remaining ingredients.
- Add the flour mixture in the bowl of the milk mixture and beat till smooth.
- Lightly, grease a skillet and heat on medium-high heat.
- Place about 1/4 C. of the mixture and tilt the pan to spread it evenly.
- Cook for about 3-4 minutes and carefully, flip it.
- Cook for about 2-3 minutes.
- Repeat with the remaining mixture.
- Serve hot.

Amount per serving (4 total)

Timing Information:

Preparation	10 m
Cooking	10 m
Total Time	2 h 20 m

Nutritional Information:

Calories	287 kcal
Fat	15.3 g
Carbohydrates	29.3g
Protein	4.4 g
Cholesterol	31 mg
Sodium	241 mg

* Percent Daily Values are based on a 2,000 calorie diet.

CREAM CHEESE CREPES

Ingredients

- 3 ounces cream cheese, softened
- 2 eggs
- 1 tsp ground cinnamon
- 1 tbsp sugar-free syrup
- 1 tsp butter

Directions

- In a bowl, crack the eggs and beat well.
- Add the cream cheese, 1 tbsp at one time and beat till well combined.
- Add the sugar-free syrup and cinnamon and beat till smooth.
- Grease a skillet with butter and heat on medium heat and then reduce the heat to medium-low.
- Place the desired amount of the mixture and tilt the pan to spread it evenly.
- Cook for about 4 minutes and carefully, flip it.
- Cook for about 1-2 minutes.
- Repeat with the remaining mixture.
- Serve hot.

Amount per serving (2 total)

Timing Information:

Preparation	5 m
Cooking	20 m
Total Time	25 m

Nutritional Information:

Calories	241 kcal
Fat	21.8 g
Carbohydrates	2.4g
Protein	9.6 g
Cholesterol	238 mg
Sodium	215 mg

* Percent Daily Values are based on a 2,000 calorie diet.

Chocolate Hazelnut Spread & Banana Filled Crepes

Ingredients

- 1 C. chocolate hazelnut spread
- 4 crepes
- 4 bananas, sliced
- 1 (7 ounce) can pressurized whipped cream

Directions

- Divide about 1/4 C. of the chocolate spread over each crepe.
- Divide the banana slices in the center of the crepes evenly and roll around the filling.
- Warm a nonstick skillet on medium heat.
- Warm each crepe roll for about 90 seconds
- Place the whipped cream over the crepes and serve.

Amount per serving (4 total)

Timing Information:

Preparation	10 m
Cooking	10 m
Total Time	20 m

Nutritional Information:

Calories	639 kcal
Fat	32.9 g
Carbohydrates	81.6g
Protein	9.7 g
Cholesterol	87 mg
Sodium	227 mg

* Percent Daily Values are based on a 2,000 calorie diet.

BERRIES FILLED CREPES

Ingredients

- 1/2 C. whole wheat flour
- 2 egg whites
- 1/2 C. skim milk
- 1 pinch salt
- 1 tbsp vegetable oil
- 1/2 C. mixed frozen berries, thawed and drained
- 1 tbsp confectioners' sugar

Directions

- In a large bowl, add all the ingredients except the berries and confectioner's sugar and beat till smooth.
- Lightly, grease a skillet and heat on medium heat.
- Place about 1/4 C. of mixture and tilt the pan to spread it evenly.
- Cook for about 2 minutes and carefully, flip it.
- Place about 2 tbsps of the berries in the center.
- Cook for about 2 minutes and roll around the berries.
- Repeat with the remaining mixture and berries.
- Serve with a dusting of confectioner's sugar.

Amount per serving (2 total)

Timing Information:

Preparation	10 m
Cooking	5 m
Total Time	15 m

Nutritional Information:

Calories	228 kcal
Fat	7.6 g
Carbohydrates	33g
Protein	10.1 g
Cholesterol	1 mg
Sodium	276 mg

* Percent Daily Values are based on a 2,000 calorie diet.

Hungarian Crepes

Ingredients

Pancakes:

- 2 C. all-purpose flour
- 2 eggs
- 1 C. milk
- 1 C. soda water
- 1/2 C. vegetable oil
- 1 pinch salt
- Almond Filling:
- 1 C. chopped almonds
- 1/2 C. white sugar
- 1/4 C. milk
- 1/4 tsp vanilla extract
- 1 1/2 tsps rum
- Chocolate Topping:
- 1/4 C. water
- 1/2 C. white sugar
- 1/2 C. chopped bittersweet chocolate
- 2 tbsps margarine

Directions

- For the crepes in a large bowl, add the eggs and flour and beat till smooth.
- Add remaining ingredients and beat till well combined.
- Refrigerate, covered for about overnight.
- Lightly, grease a skillet and heat on medium heat.
- Place about 1/4 C. of the mixture and tilt the pan to spread it evenly.

- Cook for about 1 minute per side.
- Repeat with the remaining mixture.
- For the filling, in a pan, mix together all the ingredients on low heat.
- Cook, stirring continuously till the sugar dissolves completely.
- Remove from heat and let it cool slightly.
- For topping in another pan, mix together all the ingredients except margarine on low heat.
- Cook, stirring continuously till the chocolate melts completely.
- Remove from heat and immediately, stir in the margarine till well combined.
- Divide the filling in the center of the crepes evenly and roll around the filling.
- Place the sauce over the crepes and serve.

Amount per serving (5 total)

Timing Information:

Preparation	40 m
Cooking	30 m
Total Time	9 h 10 m

Nutritional Information:

Calories	873 kcal
Fat	47.4 g
Carbohydrates	98.7g
Protein	15.1 g
Cholesterol	71 mg
Sodium	104 mg

* Percent Daily Values are based on a 2,000 calorie diet.

BACON & BANANA FILLED CREPES

Ingredients

- 1 C. milk
- 4 large eggs
- 1 tbsp butter, melted
- 1 tbsp white sugar
- 1 tsp almond extract
- 1 1/4 C. all-purpose flour
- 12 slices bacon
- 3 tbsps butter, divided

- 6 firm bananas, sliced in half lengthwise
- 12 tbsps chocolate-hazelnut spread, divided
- 12 tbsps peanut butter, divided
- 1/2 tbsp honey, divided
- 1 tsp confectioners' sugar
- 1 tbsp chocolate syrup

Directions

- In a blender, add the flour, white sugar, eggs, milk, vanilla and 1 tbsp of butter and pulse till smooth and keep aside for at least 20 minutes.
- Heat a large skillet on medium-high heat and cook the bacon for about 10 minutes.
- Transfer the bacon onto a paper towel lined plate.
- Lightly, grease a crepe pan with 1 tsp of the butter and heat on medium-high heat.

- Place about 1/4 C. of the mixture and tilt the pan to spread it evenly.
- Cook for about 2-3 minutes and carefully, flip it.
- Cook for about 1-2 minutes.
- Repeat with the remaining mixture.
- In a skillet, melt 2 tbsps of the butter and cook the banana slices for about 3 minutes per side and remove from heat.
- Spread about 1 tbsp of the hazelnut spread over each crepe, followed by 1 tbsp of peanut butter.
- Arrange a bacon slice in the center of each crepe, followed by 1 banana slice and 1/2 tsp of the honey.
- Roll each crepe around the filling.
- Serve with a sprinkling of a confectioner's sugar and a drizzling of chocolate syrup.

Amount per serving (12 total)

Timing Information:

Preparation	30 m
Cooking	45 m
Total Time	1 h 15 m

Nutritional Information:

Calories	406 kcal
Fat	22.8 g
Carbohydrates	40.3g
Protein	13.3 g
Cholesterol	84 mg
Sodium	362 mg

* Percent Daily Values are based on a 2,000 calorie diet.

CHEESY BLINTZES CREPE CASSEROLE

Ingredients

- 1/2 C. butter
- 2 (13 ounce) packages frozen cheese-filled blintzes
- 6 egg whites
- 6 egg yolks
- 2 C. sour cream
- 1/3 C. white sugar
- 1 tsp vanilla extract
- 1/2 tsp salt

Directions

- Set your oven to 350 degrees F before doing anything else.
- In a 13x9-inch baking dish, add the butter and place it in the oven for about 3 minutes.
- Remove the baking dish from the oven and arrange the blintzes in a single layer over melted butter.
- In a bowl, add the egg whites and beat till soft peaks form.
- In another bowl, add the remaining ingredients and beat till smooth.
- Gently, fold in about 1/3 of the beaten egg whites.
- Now, fold in the remaining beaten egg whites till well combined.
- Spread the crepe mixture over the blintzes evenly.
- Cook in the oven for about 45 minutes.

Amount per serving (12 total)

Timing Information:

Preparation	20 m
Cooking	45 m
Total Time	1 h 5 m

Nutritional Information:

Calories	287 kcal
Fat	19.9 g
Carbohydrates	20.7g
Protein	10.4 g
Cholesterol	155 mg
Sodium	339 mg

* Percent Daily Values are based on a 2,000 calorie diet.

Sweet & Sour Crepes

Ingredients

- 2 C. almond milk
- 2 tbsps cider vinegar
- 1/2 lemon, juiced
- 3/4 C. rice flour
- 1/3 C. potato starch
- 1/4 C. arrowroot flour
- 3 tbsps tapioca flour
- 2 tbsps coconut sugar
- 1 1/2 tsps baking powder
- 1/2 tsp baking soda
- 1/2 tsp xanthan gum
- 1/2 tsp salt
- 3 tbsps coconut oil, melted
- 2 eggs

Directions

- In a bowl, mix together almond milk, lemon juice and vinegar and keep aside for about 10 minutes. In another large bowl, mix together the remaining ingredients except the eggs and oil. Add the eggs and oil and beat till smooth. Add the almond mixture into flour mixture till well combined. Lightly, grease a skillet and heat on medium heat.
- Place about 1/4 C. of the mixture and tilt the pan to spread it evenly.
- Cook for about 2-3 minutes and carefully, flip it.
- Cook for about 2-3 minutes.
- Repeat with the remaining mixture. Serve hot.

Amount per serving (4 total)

Timing Information:

Preparation	15 m
Cooking	10 m
Total Time	35 m

Nutritional Information:

Calories	384 kcal
Fat	14.8 g
Carbohydrates	57.7g
Protein	5.6 g
Cholesterol	93 mg
Sodium	764 mg

* Percent Daily Values are based on a 2,000 calorie diet.

Easy Crepes

Ingredients

- 1 C. all-purpose flour
- 1/2 tsp white sugar
- 1/4 tsp salt
- 1 C. milk
- 1 egg

Directions

- In a large bowl, mix together the sugar, flour and salt.
- Add the egg and milk and beat till smooth.
- Lightly, grease a skillet and heat on medium-high heat.
- Place the desired amount of the mixture and tilt the pan to spread it evenly.
- Cook for about 2 minutes and carefully, flip it.
- Cook till golden brown.
- Repeat with the remaining mixture.
- Serve hot.

Amount per serving (3 total)

Timing Information:

Preparation	5 m
Cooking	5 m
Total Time	10 m

Nutritional Information:

Calories	219 kcal
Fat	3.7 g
Carbohydrates	36.4g
Protein	9.1 g
Cholesterol	69 mg
Sodium	251 mg

* Percent Daily Values are based on a 2,000 calorie diet.

Yogurt, Honey & Banana Filled Crepes

Ingredients

- 1 3/4 C. fat-free milk
- 3/4 C. flour
- 1 egg
- 1 egg white
- 2 tbsps honey, divided

- 1 (8 ounce) container low-fat banana yogurt
- 1 banana, diced
- 1/2 tsp vanilla extract
- Fresh mint sprigs
- Powdered sugar

Directions

- In a bowl, add the egg, egg whites, flour and 1 tbsp of honey and beat till well combined and keep aside for About 10 minutes.
- Lightly, grease a skillet and heat on medium heat.
- Place about 1/4 C. of the mixture and tilt the pan to spread it evenly.
- Cook everything on both sides till golden brown.
- Repeat with the remaining mixture.
- In a blender, add the remaining honey, yogurt and vanilla and pulse till smooth.
- Transfer the yogurt mixture into a bowl and fold in chopped banana.

- Divide the banana mixture in the center of the crepes evenly and roll around the filling.
- Serve with a topping of powdered sugar and mint if you like.

Amount per serving (4 total)

Timing Information:

Preparation	15 m
Cooking	15 m
Total Time	30 m

Nutritional Information:

Calories	260 kcal
Fat	1.6 g
Carbohydrates	50.6g
Protein	11.6 g
Cholesterol	44 mg
Sodium	114 mg

* Percent Daily Values are based on a 2,000 calorie diet.

CREAMY BANANA FILLED BEER CREPES

Ingredients

- 1 C. all-purpose flour
- 1 C. stale beer, room temperature
- 4 eggs, room temperature
- 2 tbsps vegetable oil
- 1/4 tsp ground nutmeg
- 1/4 tsp salt
- 4 bananas, sliced 1/4-inch thick
- 1 lemon, juiced
- 1 (8 ounce) package cream cheese
- 1/4 C. brown sugar
- 1 C. whipped topping
- 1 C. white sugar
- 1/2 C. boiling water
- 3 tbsps cornstarch
- 1/2 C. water
- 3 tbsps butter
- 8 tsps vegetable oil, divided

Directions

- In a large bowl, add the flour, nutmeg, salt, eggs, beer and 2 tbsps of oil and beat till smooth.
- In a second bowl, add the sliced banana and lemon juice and toss to coat well.
- In a third bowl, add the brown sugar and cream cheese and beat till fluffy and light.

- Gently, fold in the whipped topping.
- In a pan, add the white sugar on medium heat and cook, stirring continuously for about 2-4 minutes till melted.
- Remove the pan from heat and immediately, stir in boiling water.
- Return the pan on heat and cook, stirring till a clear syrup forms.
- In a small bowl, mix together the water and cornstarch.
- Slowly, add the cornstarch mixture in the pa, beating continuously and reduce the heat to low.
- Simmer, stirring continuously for about 5-7 minutes.
- Add the butter and beat till a caramel sauce forms.
- Grease a crepe pan with 1 tsp of oil and heat on medium heat.
- Place about 1/4 C. of the mixture and tilt the pan to spread it evenly.
- Cook everything on both sides till golden brown.
- Repeat with the remaining mixture.
- Place about 2 tbsps of the caramel sauce in the center of each crepe, followed by cream cheese mixture and banana slices and roll around the filling.
- Serve with a drizzling of the remaining caramel sauce.

Amount per serving (8 total)

Timing Information:

Preparation	1 h
Cooking	30 m
Total Time	1 h 30 m

Nutritional Information:

Calories	516 kcal
Fat	27 g
Carbohydrates	61.3g
Protein	7.7 g
Cholesterol	135 mg
Sodium	231 mg

* Percent Daily Values are based on a 2,000 calorie diet.

Apple Filled Crepes

Ingredients

- 3 eggs
- 1/4 tsp salt
- 2 C. all-purpose flour
- 2 C. milk
- 1/4 C. vegetable oil
- 1/2 tsp ground cinnamon
- 4 Granny Smith apples, peeled and diced
- 1/2 C. white sugar
- 2 tsps cinnamon
- 2 tbsps water
- 2 tbsps cornstarch
- 1 tbsp water
- 1 1/2 tbsps milk
- 8 tsps vegetable oil, divided

Directions

- In a bowl, add the eggs and salt and beat well.
- Slowly, add the flour, beating continuously, followed by 2 C. of milk till well combined.
- Add 1/4 C. of the oil and 1/2 tsp of the cinnamon and beat till smooth and refrigerate, covered for at least 1 hour.
- In another bowl, mix together the apples, 2 tbsps of the water, sugar and the remaining cinnamon.

- In a small bowl, mix together the cornstarch and remaining water and transfer the mixture into the bowl of the apples mixture.
- In a pan, add the apples mixture on medium heat and cook, stirring occasionally for about 8-10 minutes.
- Grease a crepe pan with 1 tsp of oil and heat on medium heat.
- Place about 1/3 C. of the mixture and tilt the pan to spread it evenly.
- Cook for about 30 seconds and carefully, flip it.
- Cook till golden brown.
- Repeat with the remaining mixture.
- Divide the apple mixture in the center of the crepes evenly and roll around the filling.
- Serve immediately.

Amount per serving (8 total)

Timing Information:

Preparation	30 m
Cooking	30 m
Total Time	2 h

Nutritional Information:

Calories	361 kcal
Fat	14.8 g
Carbohydrates	50.4g
Protein	7.9 g
Cholesterol	75 mg
Sodium	127 mg

* Percent Daily Values are based on a 2,000 calorie diet.

Nutmeg Coconut Filled Crepes

Ingredients

- 1 1/2 C. all-purpose flour
- 1 tbsp white sugar
- 1/2 tsp baking powder
- 1/2 tsp salt
- 2 C. milk
- 2 tbsps butter, melted
- 2 eggs
- 1/2 tsp vanilla extract
- 2 tsps vegetable oil
- 1/2 C. flaked coconut
- 1 tbsp white sugar
- 1/4 tsp ground cardamom

Directions

- In a large bowl, sift together 1 tbsp of the sugar, flour, baking powder and salt. Add butter, milk, eggs and vanilla and beat till smooth.
- Lightly, grease a skillet with vegetable oil and heat on medium-high heat. Place about 1/4 C. of the mixture and tilt the pan to spread it evenly. Cook for about 2 minutes and carefully, flip it.
- Cook for about 2 minutes.
- Repeat with the remaining mixture.
- In a bowl, mix together the remaining ingredients.
- Divide the coconut mixture in the center of the crepes evenly and roll around the filling and serve.

Amount per serving (8 total)

Timing Information:

Preparation	10 m
Cooking	15 m
Total Time	25 m

Nutritional Information:

Calories	203 kcal
Fat	8 g
Carbohydrates	26.5g
Protein	6.2 g
Cholesterol	59 mg
Sodium	252 mg

* Percent Daily Values are based on a 2,000 calorie diet.

ANISE & ORANGE CREPES

Ingredients

- 4 large eggs
- 1 C. milk
- 3/4 C. orange juice
- 1 tbsp anise extract
- 1 C. all-purpose flour
- 2 tbsps butter, divided
- Sugar, for dusting

Directions

- In a large bowl, add all the ingredients except butter and sugar and beat till smooth.
- Lightly, grease a skillet with butter and heat on medium-high heat.
- Place about 1/4 C. of the mixture and tilt the pan to spread it evenly.
- Cook for about 2 minutes per side.
- Repeat with the remaining mixture.
- Serve with a sprinkling of a sugar.

Amount per serving (6 total)

Timing Information:

Preparation	10 m
Cooking	10 m
Total Time	8 h 20 m

Nutritional Information:

Calories	213 kcal
Fat	8.2 g
Carbohydrates	25.5g
Protein	7.9 g
Cholesterol	137 mg
Sodium	91 mg

* Percent Daily Values are based on a 2,000 calorie diet.

Choco Hazelnut Banana Filled Crepes

Ingredients

Crepe Batter:

- 1/2 C. whole or milk
- 1 1/2 tbsps melted butter
- 1 egg yolk
- 1 tsp vanilla
- 2 tsps hazelnut liqueur
- 1 tbsp cocoa
- 2 tbsps confectioners' sugar
- 1/3 C. white flour

Chocolate Sauce:

- 1/2 tbsp butter
- 1 tbsp whole or milk
- 2 tsps hazelnut liqueur
- 1 tbsp cocoa
- 2 tbsps confectioners' sugar
- 2 ripe bananas, sliced

Directions

- In a large bowl, add the egg yolk, 1 1/2 tbsps of melted butter, 1/2 C. of milk, 2 tsps of hazelnut liqueur and vanilla and mix well.
- Add the cocoa powder and beat till well combined.
- Add the confectioner's sugar and beat till well combined.
- Slowly, add the flour, beating continuously till well combined and keep aside.

- In a pan, melt the remaining butter on low heat and stir in the remaining ingredients except banana slices.
- Keep the pan on very low heat to keep it warm.
- Lightly, grease a crepe pan and heat on medium heat.
- Place about 1/4 C. of the mixture and tilt the pan to spread it evenly.
- Cook for about 2 minutes and carefully, flip it.
- Cook for about 1 minute.
- Repeat with the remaining mixture.
- In serving plates, arrange the crepes.
- Place about 1/4 of the banana slices over each crepe and top with sauce evenly.
- Roll the crepes around the filling and serve with a sprinkling of a confectioner's sugar.

Amount per serving (4 total)

Timing Information:

Preparation	20 m
Cooking	10 m
Total Time	30 m

Nutritional Information:

Calories	236 kcal
Fat	8.6 g
Carbohydrates	35.1g
Protein	4.1 g
Cholesterol	70 mg
Sodium	58 mg

* Percent Daily Values are based on a 2,000 calorie diet.

SAUSAGE & VEGGIE FILLED CREPES

Ingredients

- 1 pound ground pork sausage
- 1 small onion, diced
- 1 red bell peppers, seeded and diced
- 2 C. fresh mushrooms, sliced
- 1/4 C. cilantro, finely chopped
- 5 eggs
- 6 egg whites
- 1/4 C. milk
- 1 C. shredded Cheddar cheese
- salt and pepper to taste
- 6 egg yolks
- 3/4 C. butter
- 2 lemons, juiced
- 1 C. all-purpose flour
- 1 egg
- 2 C. milk
- 1 pinch paprika
- 1 (16 ounce) jar salsa

Directions

- Heat a large nonstick skillet on medium heat and cook the sausage till half cooked and then discard most of the fat.
- Add the mushrooms, bell peppers and onion and cook till the vegetables become tender.
- Remove the sausage mixture from skillet, leaving a little fat in the skillet.

- In a bowl, add 1/4 C. of the milk, 5 eggs, egg whites and cheese and beat till well combined.
- In the same skillet, add the egg mixture on medium-high heat and cook, stirring continuously till eggs become set.
- Mix together the butter, egg yolks and lemon juice in a double boiler on medium heat.
- Cook, beating continuously till the butter melts completely and remove from heat and keep aside.
- In a bowl, add the flour, milk and remaining egg and beat till well combined.
- Strain the egg mixture through a fine sieve.
- Lightly, grease a crepe pan and heat on medium-high heat.
- Place about 1/3 C. of the mixture and tilt the pan to spread it evenly.
- Cook everything on both sides till golden brown.
- Repeat with the remaining mixture.
- Divide the sausage mixture in the center of the crepes evenly and roll around the filling.
- Place the egg yolk sauce over the crepes and top with a sprinkling of paprika.
- Serve these crepe rolls with salsa.

Amount per serving (7 total)

Timing Information:

Preparation	30 m
Cooking	20 m
Total Time	50 m

Nutritional Information:

Calories	774 kcal
Fat	61.4 g
Carbohydrates	30g
Protein	29.2 g
Cholesterol	455 mg
Sodium	11329 mg

* Percent Daily Values are based on a 2,000 calorie diet.

BEER CREPES

Ingredients

- 3 eggs, lightly beaten
- 1 C. milk
- 1 C. beer, optional
- 1 3/4 C. all-purpose flour
- 1 pinch salt
- 2 tbsps vegetable oil
- 2 tbsps butter

Directions

- In a large bowl, add the beer, milk and eggs and beat till smooth.
- Slowly, add flour, beating continuously till well combined.
- Add oil and salt and beat till smooth.
- Lightly, grease a skillet with butter and heat on medium heat.
- Place about 1/3 C. of the mixture and tilt the pan to spread it evenly.
- Cook for about 1-2 minutes and carefully, flip it.
- Cook for about 30 seconds.
- Repeat with the remaining mixture.
- Serve hot.

Amount per serving (12 total)

Timing Information:

Preparation	1 h
Cooking	3 m
Total Time	1 h 15 m

Nutritional Information:

Calories	140 kcal
Fat	6 g
Carbohydrates	15.7g
Protein	4.2 g
Cholesterol	53 mg
Sodium	41 mg

* Percent Daily Values are based on a 2,000 calorie diet.

Spiced Flax Seeds Crepes

Ingredients

- 3 eggs
- 1 C. soy milk
- 1/4 C. olive oil
- 1/2 C. all-purpose flour
- 1/4 C. whole wheat flour

- 2 tbsps flax seeds
- 1/4 tsp salt
- 1/4 tsp ground cinnamon
- 1/8 tsp ground nutmeg
- 1 tsp vegetable oil

Directions

- In a large bowl, add the soy milk, olive oil and eggs and beat till well combined.
- In another bowl, add the remaining ingredients except vegetable oil and beat till smooth.
- Add the flour mixture into egg mixture and beat till well combined.
- Lightly, grease a skillet and heat on medium heat.
- Place about 1/4 of the mixture and tilt the pan to spread it evenly.
- Cook for about 3-4 minutes and carefully, flip it.
- Cook for about 1-2 minutes.
- Repeat with the remaining mixture.

Amount per serving (4 total)

Timing Information:

Preparation	10 m
Cooking	10 m
Total Time	20 m

Nutritional Information:

Calories	331 kcal
Fat	22.3 g
Carbohydrates	23.4g
Protein	10.5 g
Cholesterol	140 mg
Sodium	232 mg

* Percent Daily Values are based on a 2,000 calorie diet.

CURRIED CHICKEN & OLIVES FILLED CREPES

Ingredients

CREPES

- 1 1/2 C. all-purpose flour
- 2 1/2 C. milk
- 3 eggs, beaten
- 2 tbsps vegetable oil
- 1/2 tsp salt

FILLING

- 1/4 C. butter
- 1 1/4 C. diced celery
- 1 C. diced onion

- 2 tbsps all-purpose flour
- 1 tsp salt
- 3/4 tsp curry powder
- 1 C. milk
- 2 cubes chicken bouillon
- 1/2 C. warm water
- 3/4 C. sliced black olives
- 2 1/2 C. cooked, diced chicken breast meat
- 1/4 C. freshly grated Parmesan cheese

Directions

- Set your oven to 400 degrees F before doing anything else.
- For the crepes, in a large bowl, add the all the ingredients and beat till smooth.
- Lightly, grease a skillet and heat on medium heat.

- Place the desired amount of the mixture and tilt the pan to spread it evenly.
- Cook till golden brown from one side.
- Repeat with the remaining mixture.
- For the filling, in a large skillet, melt the butter on medium heat and sauté the onion and celery till tender.
- Stir in the flour, curry powder and salt till well combined.
- In a bowl, mix together the warm water and bouillon.
- Add the bouillon mixture and milk in the skillet, stirring continuously till the mixture becomes thick.
- Stir in chicken and olives.
- Divide the filling mixture in the center of the crepes evenly and roll around the filling.
- Arrange the crepe rolls, seam side down into a 13x9-inch baking dish in a single layer.
- Place the cheese over rolls evenly and cook in the oven for about 12 minutes.

Amount per serving (7 total)

Timing Information:

Preparation	30 m
Cooking	15 m
Total Time	45 m

Nutritional Information:

Calories	430 kcal
Fat	21.2 g
Carbohydrates	32g
Protein	27.1 g
Cholesterol	155 mg
Sodium	1185 mg

* Percent Daily Values are based on a 2,000 calorie diet.

CRACKER FILLED CREPES

Ingredients

- 2 tbsps millet flour
- 2 tbsps soy milk
- 1/2 tsp vegetable oil
- 1 tbsp Chinese black bean sauce
- 1 tsp water
- 1/2 tsp Asian chile pepper sauce
- 1 tsp water
- cooking spray
- 1 egg, beaten
- 1/2 green onion, sliced
- 1 tbsp torn fresh cilantro leaves
- 2 whole crackers

Directions

- In a large bowl, add the millet flour, oil and soy milk and beat till creamy (You can use 1 tsp of water to thin the mixture)
- In a bowl, add the black bean sauce and 1 tsp of water and mash completely.
- In another bowl, mix together the chile pepper sauce and remaining water.
- Lightly, grease a skillet and heat on medium-low heat.
- Place the desired amount of the mixture and tilt the pan to spread it evenly.

- Cook for about 1-2 minutes and place the beaten egg on top evenly.
- Cook for about 1-2 minutes more and place the cilantro and green onion on top evenly, pressing gently.
- Carefully, flip it and spread the both sauces on top evenly.
- Place the crackers in the center and roll around crackers tightly.
- Serve hot.

Amount per serving (1 total)

Timing Information:

Preparation	15 m
Cooking	5 m
Total Time	20 m

Nutritional Information:

Calories	220 kcal
Fat	11.2 g
Carbohydrates	20.1g
Protein	10.1 g
Cholesterol	186 mg
Sodium	266 mg

* Percent Daily Values are based on a 2,000 calorie diet.

BACON & VEGGIE FILLED CREPES

Ingredients

- 1 recipe Basic Crepes
- 6 slices bacon
- 1 tbsp unsalted butter
- 1/2 pound fresh mushrooms, sliced
- 3 tbsps unsalted butter
- 1/4 C. all-purpose flour
- 1 C. milk
- 1 (10 ounce) package frozen chopped spinach, thawed and drained
- 1 tbsp chopped fresh parsley
- 2 tbsps grated Parmesan cheese
- salt and pepper to taste
- 2/3 C. chicken broth
- 2 eggs
- 1/2 C. lemon juice
- salt and pepper to taste

Directions

- Prepare the crepes from the basic crepe recipe.
- Heat a large nonstick skillet on medium-high heat and cook the bacon till browned completely.
- Remove the bacon, leaving about 1 tbsp of bacon fat in the skillet.

- Place the bacon onto a paper towel lined plate to drain and then crumble it.
- Add 1 tbsp of the butter and sauté mushrooms till desired doneness.
- In a large pan, melt the remaining butter on medium heat and add flour, stirring continuously till smooth.
- Slowly, add the milk, beating continuously till the mixture becomes thick.
- Stir in the mushrooms, bacon, Parmesan, spinach, parsley, salt and black pepper and cook for about 10 minutes.
- Meanwhile in another pan, add the broth and bring to a boil
- In a bowl, add the eggs and lemon juice and beat till well combined.
- Slowly, add the broth, beating continuously and season with salt and black pepper.
- Divide the bacon mixture in the center of the crepes evenly and roll around the filling.
- Serve the crepe rolls with the egg sauce.

Amount per serving (4 total)

Timing Information:

Preparation	35 m
Cooking	20 m
Total Time	1 h 5 m

Nutritional Information:

Calories	445 kcal
Fat	35.6 g
Carbohydrates	17.9g
Protein	15.9 g
Cholesterol	160 mg
Sodium	785 mg

* Percent Daily Values are based on a 2,000 calorie diet.

Zucchini Blossom Filled Crepes

Ingredients

- 2 eggs
- 3 C. skim milk
- 1/4 tsp salt
- 1 tsp melted butter
- 2 C. all-purpose flour
- 2 tbsps butter
- 1 clove garlic, minced
- 1 onion, finely diced
- 1 C. chicken broth
- 1 pound zucchini blossoms, rinsed and chopped
- 1 large tomato, seeded and diced
- 1 pinch ground nutmeg, or to taste
- 1 tbsp chopped fresh epazote leaves
- 1 (8 ounce) container crème fraiche
- salt and black pepper to taste
- 2 C. half-and-half cream
- 1 C. grated Manchego cheese

Directions

- Set your oven to 350 degrees F before doing anything else.
- In a blender, add the melted butter, eggs, milk, flour and salt and pulse till well combined.
- Lightly, grease a skillet and heat on medium heat.

- Place the desired amount of the mixture and tilt the pan to spread it evenly.
- Cook everything on both sides till golden brown.
- Repeat with the remaining mixture.
- In a skillet, melt the butter on medium heat and sauté onion and garlic for about 5 minutes.
- Stir in the broth and simmer till reduces to half.
- Stir in the zucchini blossoms and cook, covered till softened.
- Stir in the tomato, epazote and nutmeg and cook for about 2 minutes.
- Stir in the crème fraiche, salt and black pepper and remove from heat.
- Divide the zucchini mixture in the center of the crepes evenly and roll around the filling.
- Arrange the crepe rolls, seam side down into a 13x9-inch baking dish in a single layer.
- Place the half-and-half over rolls evenly followed by cheese.
- With foil, cover the baking dish and cook in the oven for about 10 minutes.

Amount per serving (6 total)

Timing Information:

Preparation	25 m
Cooking	1 h 5 m
Total Time	1 h 30 m

Nutritional Information:

Calories	594 kcal
Fat	35.4 g
Carbohydrates	51.3g
Protein	19.6 g
Cholesterol	174 mg
Sodium	678 mg

* Percent Daily Values are based on a 2,000 calorie diet.

CURRIED CHICKEN FILLED CREPES

Ingredients

- 1/2 C. condensed cream of chicken soup
- 2 1/2 tbsps mayonnaise
- 2 1/2 tbsps heavy whipping cream
- 1 1/2 tbsps grated onion
- 1 1/2 tsps lemon juice
- 1 tsp curry powder
- salt and ground black pepper to taste
- 2 1/2 C. chopped cooked chicken
- 8 crepes
- 1 C. firmly packed grated Cheddar cheese
- 1/3 C. heavy whipping cream

Directions

- Set your oven to 390 degrees F before doing anything else and lightly grease a baking dish.
- In a large bowl, add the chicken soup, 2 1/2 tbsps of whipping cream, mayonnaise, lemon juice, onion, curry powder, salt and black pepper together and mix till well combined.
- Stir in the chicken.
- Divide the chicken mixture in the center of the crepes evenly and roll around the filling.

- Arrange the crepe rolls, seam side down onto the prepared baking dish in a single layer.
- Place the cheese over the rolls evenly followed by the remaining whipping cream and cook everything in the oven for about 25-30 minutes.

Amount per serving (8 total)

Timing Information:

Preparation	25 m
Cooking	30 m
Total Time	55 m

Nutritional Information:

Calories	462 kcal
Fat	27.5 g
Carbohydrates	24.6g
Protein	27.8 g
Cholesterol	239 mg
Sodium	332 mg

* Percent Daily Values are based on a 2,000 calorie diet.

PALEO CREPES

Ingredients

- 4 egg whites
- 3 tbsps almond milk
- 1/4 tsp vanilla extract
- 2 tbsps coconut flour
- 1/8 tsp baking powder
- 1 pinch sea salt

Directions

- In a large bowl, add all the almond milk, egg whites and vanilla and beat till smooth.
- Add the remaining ingredients and beat till smooth and keep aside for about 8 minutes.
- Lightly, grease a skillet and heat on medium-high heat.
- Place about 1/3 of the mixture and tilt the pan to spread it evenly.
- Cook for about 2 minutes and carefully, flip it.
- Cook for about 1-2 minutes or till golden brown.
- Repeat with the remaining mixture.
- Serve hot.

Amount per serving (3 total)

Timing Information:

Preparation	10 m
Cooking	5 m
Total Time	23 m

Nutritional Information:

Calories	66 kcal
Fat	1.2 g
Carbohydrates	7.6g
Protein	6.3 g
Cholesterol	0 mg
Sodium	211 mg

* Percent Daily Values are based on a 2,000 calorie diet.

CHICKEN FILLED CREPES

Ingredients

- 3 recipes Basic Crepes
- 4 tbsps butter
- 2 tbsps finely chopped onion
- 4 tbsps all-purpose flour
- 1 C. milk
- 3/4 C. chicken broth
- 1/4 C. dry white wine
- 1/4 tsp chopped dried tarragon
- 2 egg yolks
- 2 C. diced cooked chicken
- salt to taste
- 1/4 C. milk

Directions

- Set your oven to 350 degrees F before doing anything else and lightly, grease a 13x9-inch baking dish.
- Prepare the crepes from the basic crepe recipe.
- In a pan, melt the butter on medium heat and sauté onion for about 2 minutes.
- Stir in the flour and then slowly, add 1 C. of milk, beating continuously till smooth.
- Reduce the heat to medium-low and stir in wine, broth and tarragon.
- Cook for about 4 minutes.

- In a bowl, beat the egg yolks.
- Slowly, add about 3 tbsps of the milk mixture, beating continuously.
- Add the egg yolk mixture in the pan, beating continuously and cook for about 1 minute, then remove everything from the heat
- In a bowl mix together half of the sauce with the cooked chicken and salt.
- Divide the chicken mixture in the center of the crepes evenly and roll around the filling.
- Arrange the crepe rolls, seam side down into prepared baking dish in a single layer.
- In a bowl, add the remaining sauce and 1/4 C. of the milk and mix well.
- Place the sauce over the rolls evenly and cook them in the oven for about 20 minutes.

Amount per serving (12 total)

Timing Information:

Preparation	20 m
Cooking	35 m
Total Time	55 m

Nutritional Information:

Calories	114 kcal
Fat	6.9 g
Carbohydrates	3.6g
Protein	8.1 g
Cholesterol	64 mg
Sodium	114 mg

* Percent Daily Values are based on a 2,000 calorie diet.

CREAM CHEESE FILLING FOR THE CREPES,

Ingredients

- 1 (8 ounce) container vegan cream cheese substitute
- 2 tbsps white sugar
- 1 tsp vanilla extract
- 1 1/2 tbsps coconut milk

Directions

- In a large bowl, add all the ingredients except oil and beat till creamy and smooth.

Amount per serving (10 total)

Timing Information:

Preparation	5 m
Cooking	5 m
Total Time	10 m

Nutritional Information:

Calories	79 kcal
Fat	6.8 g
Carbohydrates	3.4g
Protein	0.8 g
Cholesterol	0 mg
Sodium	107 mg

* Percent Daily Values are based on a 2,000 calorie diet.

Soft Crepes

Ingredients

- 1 1/2 C. all-purpose flour
- 1 C. milk
- 2 eggs
- 3 tbsps butter, melted
- 1 tbsp white sugar
- 1 dash vanilla extract
- 1 C. milk
- cooking spray

Directions

- In a large bowl, add the eggs, 1 C. of milk and flour and beat till well combined.
- Add the sugar, butter and vanilla and beat well.
- Add the remaining milk and beat till smooth.
- Lightly, grease a skillet with cooking spray and heat on medium heat.
- Place about 1/4 C. of the mixture and tilt the pan to spread it evenly.
- Cook for about 3-4 minutes and carefully, flip it.
- Cook for about 2-3 minutes or till golden brown.
- Repeat with the remaining mixture.

Amount per serving (4 total)

Timing Information:

Preparation	10 m
Cooking	30 m
Total Time	40 m

Nutritional Information:

Calories	357 kcal
Fat	14.1 g
Carbohydrates	44.8g
Protein	12.1 g
Cholesterol	126 mg
Sodium	147 mg

* Percent Daily Values are based on a 2,000 calorie diet.

LAYERED CHOCOLATE CREPE CAKE

Ingredients

Crepes:

- 2 C. milk
- 1 1/2 C. all-purpose flour
- 1/2 C. unsweetened cocoa powder
- 6 tsps confectioners' sugar
- 2 large eggs
- 1/2 tsp vanilla extract
- 1/4 tsp Kosher Salt
- 2 tbsps butter

Salted Chocolate Orange Sauce:

- 9 ounces dark chocolate, chopped
- 1 1/2 C. heavy cream
- 6 fluid ounces orange juice concentrate, undiluted
- 1/4 C. sugar
- 1 tsp vanilla
- 1/4 tsp Kosher Salt
- 2 C. heavy whipping cream

Directions

- For the crepes, in a large bowl, add all the ingredients except butter and beat till smooth.
- Grease a skillet with 1/3 tsp of butter and heat on medium-high heat.
- Place about 1/4 C. of the mixture and tilt the pan to spread it evenly.
- Cook till the top becomes bubbly and carefully, flip it.

- Cook for about 1 minute.
- Repeat with the remaining mixture.
- For the sauce, in a pan, heat the cream.
- Remove from heat and immediately, stir in chocolate till well combined.
- Stir in the remaining ingredients except whipping cream till well combined.
- In a bowl, add the whipped cream and beat till stiff.
- Spread a thin layer over 1 crepe evenly and place another crepe on top.
- Repeat this process by placing the crepes over the first layer.
- Place the layered crepe cakes over a large plate.
- With a knife, cut the cake into the desired sized wedges.
- Divide the remaining sauce into serving plates.
- Place the crepe cake wedges over the sauce.
- Serve with a topping of your choice like shaved chocolate, mint sprigs or orange sections.

Amount per serving (6 total)

Timing Information:

Preparation	15 m
Cooking	1 h
Total Time	1 h 15 m

Nutritional Information:

Calories	1035 kcal
Fat	73.6 g
Carbohydrates	185.3g
Protein	15.5 g
Cholesterol	271 mg
Sodium	303 mg

* Percent Daily Values are based on a 2,000 calorie diet.

Russian Styled Pancakes

Ingredients

- 4 1/4 C. milk
- 5 eggs
- 1/3 tsp salt
- 2 tbsps white sugar
- 1/2 tsp baking soda

- 1/8 tsp citric acid powder
- 4 C. all-purpose flour
- 3 tbsps vegetable oil
- 1 C. boiling water
- 2/3 C. butter, divided

Directions

- In a large bowl, add the eggs and milk and beat till well combined.
- Add the white sugar, flour, baking powder, salt and citric acid powder and beat till smooth. Add the boiling water and oil and mix till well combined and keep aside for at least 20 minutes. Grease a skillet with 1 tbsp of butter and heat on medium-high heat. Remove the skillet from the heat and place the desired amount of the mixture and tilt the pan to spread it evenly. Cook for about 90 seconds and carefully, flip it.
- Cook for about 1 minute.
- Repeat with the remaining mixture.
- Place your favorite filling in the center of the crepes evenly and roll around the filling.

Amount per serving (8 total)

Timing Information:

Preparation	15 m
Cooking	30 m
Total Time	1 h 5 m

Nutritional Information:

Calories	525 kcal
Fat	26.4 g
Carbohydrates	57.1g
Protein	14.4 g
Cholesterol	153 mg
Sodium	378 mg

* Percent Daily Values are based on a 2,000 calorie diet.

MOIST PANCAKES

Ingredients

- 4 eggs
- 1 C. milk
- 1/2 C. warm water
- 3 tbsps white sugar
- 1 C. all-purpose flour
- 1/2 tsp salt
- 1/2 C. butter, melted
- 1 tbsp butter

Directions

- In a large bowl, add the flour, white sugar, salt, warm water, milk and eggs and beat till smooth.
- Slowly, add the melted butter, beating continuously till well combined.
- Lightly, grease a crepe pan with the remaining butter and heat on medium heat.
- Add the required amount of mixture and tilt the pan to spread it evenly.
- Cook for about 1-2 minutes and carefully, flip it.
- Cook till golden brown.

- Repeat with the remaining mixture.
- Serve hot.

Amount per serving (4 total)

Timing Information:

Preparation	10 m
Cooking	5 m
Total Time	15 m

Nutritional Information:

Calories	481 kcal
Fat	32.4 g
Carbohydrates	36.5g
Protein	11.8 g
Cholesterol	260 mg
Sodium	571 mg

* Percent Daily Values are based on a 2,000 calorie diet.

Meat Filled Crepes Casserole

Ingredients

- 2 eggs
- 2/3 C. milk
- 1 tbsp butter, melted
- 1/2 C. all-purpose flour
- 1/4 tsp salt
- 1/4 pound ground veal
- 1/4 pound ground chicken
- 1/2 pound ground beef
- 2 tbsps butter
- 1 tbsp minced fresh parsley
- 1/2 C. grated Parmesan cheese
- 1/2 tsp salt
- 1 dash ground black pepper
- 1 dash ground nutmeg
- 2 tbsps butter
- 2 tbsps all-purpose flour
- 1 C. milk
- 1/4 tsp salt
- 1/8 tsp ground black pepper
- 1/8 tsp ground nutmeg
- 1 (32 ounce) jar tomato pasta sauce
- 1 (16 ounce) package shredded mozzarella cheese
- 1/4 C. grated Parmesan cheese

Directions

- For the crepes, in a medium bowl, crack the eggs and beat well, then mix in the butter and milk.

- Add the flour and salt and beat till well combined. (For a better result, keep the mixture aside for at least 30 minutes before cooking)
- In a lightly, greased skillet, cook the crepes till golden brown in about 6-8 inches size.
- Set your oven to 375 degrees F.
- For the filling, in a skillet, melt the butter on medium-high heat.
- Add the meat and cook till browned completely.
- Stir in the Parmesan and parsley and remove from heat and keep aside to cool.
- For the sauce, in a pan, mix together the butter and flour on medium heat and cook, stirring continuously for about 5 minutes.
- Stir in the nutmeg, salt and pepper, then slowly, add the milk and cook, stirring continuously till the desired thickness.
- In the bottom of a 13x9-inch baking dish, spread the half of the pasta sauce evenly.
- Divide the meat mixture in each crepe evenly and fold the all sides to form a roll.
- Place the crepe rolls over the pasta sauce, seam side down.
- Place the remaining pasta sauce over the rolls evenly, followed by the white sauce, mozzarella and Parmesan.
- Cook in the oven for about 20-30 minutes.

Amount per serving (8 total)

Timing Information:

Preparation	45 m
Cooking	30 m
Total Time	1 h 15 m

Nutritional Information:

Calories	557 kcal
Fat	30.1 g
Carbohydrates	39.3g
Protein	32.5 g
Cholesterol	145 mg
Sodium	1423 mg

* Percent Daily Values are based on a 2,000 calorie diet.

Maple Fruity Compote

Ingredients

- 3 tbsps butter
- 2 tbsps maple sugar
- 2 tsps grated fresh ginger
- 1 tsp ground cinnamon
- 1/2 tsp freshly grated nutmeg
- 3 C. frozen peach slices
- 1 C. frozen blackberries

Directions

- In a pan, melt the butter on medium heat.
- Add the ginger, maple syrup and spices and stir to combine.
- Stir in the peach slices and cook, stirring occasionally for about 20 minutes.
- Gently, stir in the blackberries and cook for about 5 minutes.

Amount per serving (6 total)

Timing Information:

Preparation	5 m
Cooking	25 m
Total Time	30 m

Nutritional Information:

Calories	100 kcal
Fat	6 g
Carbohydrates	12.1g
Protein	0.4 g
Cholesterol	15 mg
Sodium	44 mg

* Percent Daily Values are based on a 2,000 calorie diet.

Yeast-Vanilla Pancakes

Ingredients

- 4 C. all-purpose flour
- 4 C. lukewarm milk
- 2 large eggs, whisked
- 1/4 C. unsalted butter, melted
- 2 tbsps vegetable oil
- 1 tbsp vanilla extract
- 2 tsps bread machine yeast
- 1 1/2 tsps salt

Directions

- In a large bowl, add the flour and slowly, add the milk, beating continuously till well combined.
- Add the oil, butter and eggs and beat till smooth.
- Add the yeast, vanilla and salt and stir to combine.
- With a plastic wrap, cover the bowl and keep in warm place for about 1-3 hours till it doubles.
- Lightly, grease a griddle and heat on medium-high heat.
- Place about 1/4 C. of the mixture and tilt the pan to spread it evenly.
- Cook for about 3-4 minutes and carefully, flip it.
- Cook for about 2-3 minutes.
- Repeat with the remaining mixture.

- Serve hot.

Amount per serving (10 total)

Timing Information:

Preparation	15 m
Cooking	15 m
Total Time	1 h 30 m

Nutritional Information:

Calories	316 kcal
Fat	10.8 g
Carbohydrates	43.3g
Protein	10 g
Cholesterol	57 mg
Sodium	405 mg

* Percent Daily Values are based on a 2,000 calorie diet.

THANKS FOR READING! NOW LET'S TRY SOME SUSHI AND DUMP DINNERS....

http://bit.ly/2443TFg

To grab this **box set** simply follow the link mentioned above, or tap the book cover.

This will take you to a page where you can simply enter your email address and a PDF version of the **box set** will be emailed to you.

I hope you are ready for some serious cooking!

http://bit.ly/2443TFg

You will also receive updates about all my new books when they are free.

Also don't forget to like and subscribe on the social networks. I love meeting my readers. Links to all my profiles are below so please click and connect :)

Facebook

Twitter

COME ON...
LET'S BE FRIENDS :)

I adore my readers and love connecting with them socially. Please follow the links below so we can connect on Facebook, Twitter, and Google+.

Facebook

Twitter

I also have a blog that I regularly update for my readers so check it out below.

My Blog

CAN I ASK A FAVOUR?

If you found this book interesting, or have otherwise found any benefit in it. Then may I ask that you post a review of it on Amazon? Nothing excites me more than new reviews, especially reviews which suggest new topics for writing. I do read all reviews and I always factor feedback into my newer works.

So if you are willing to take ten minutes to write what you sincerely thought about this book then please visit our Amazon page and post your opinions.

Again thank you!

Interested in Other Easy Cookbooks?

Everything is easy! Check out my Amazon Author page for more great cookbooks:

For a complete listing of all my books please see my author page.

Printed in Great Britain
by Amazon